INTRICATE FACES
COLORING BOOK

BOOK 1

by OLAN ORIG

Intricate Faces Coloring Book, Book 1
© 2018 Olan Orig

olanorig@gmail.com

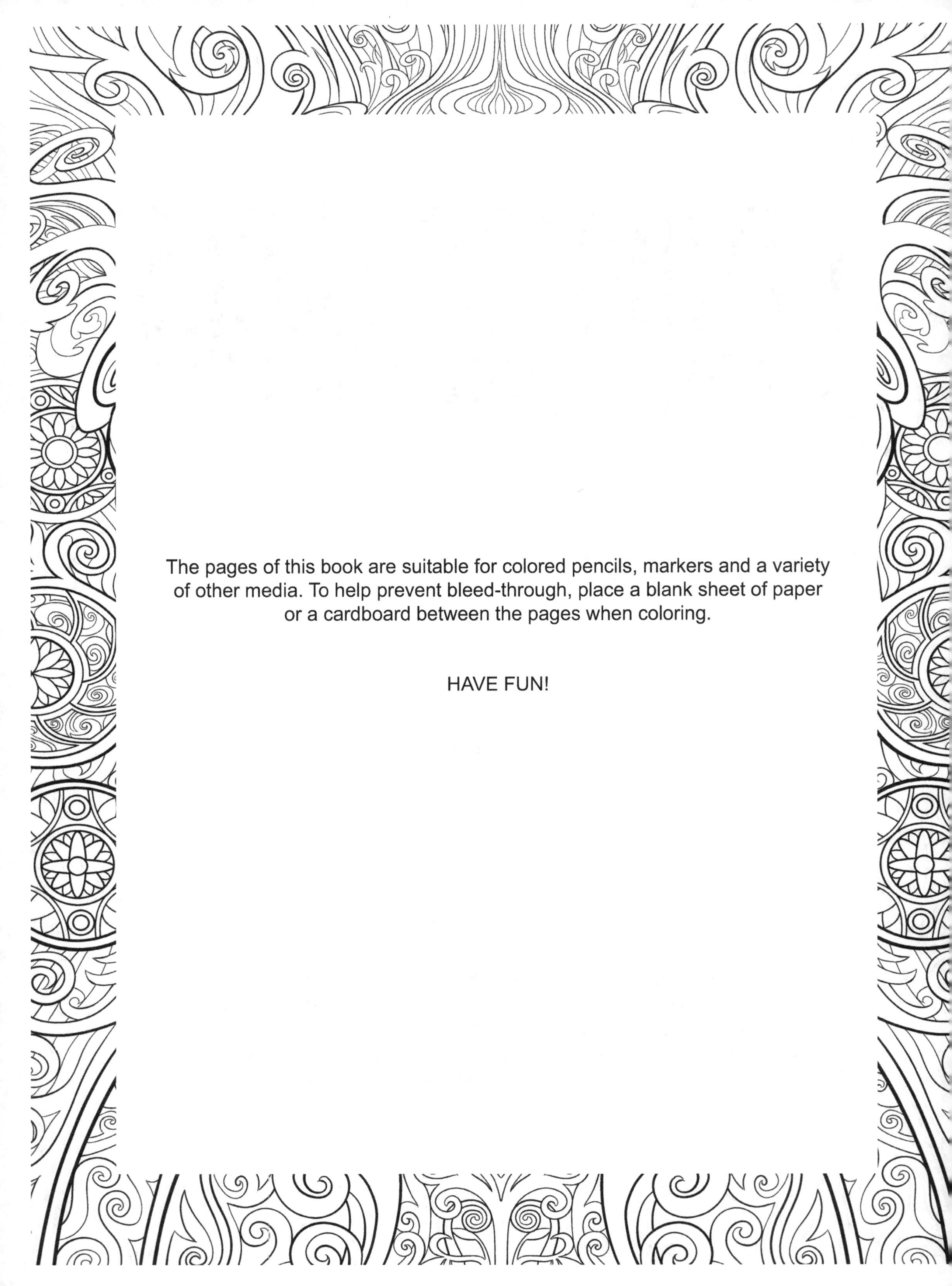

The pages of this book are suitable for colored pencils, markers and a variety of other media. To help prevent bleed-through, place a blank sheet of paper or a cardboard between the pages when coloring.

HAVE FUN!

9 781729 722138